A Coloring Book of Rappers

by Jake Franssen

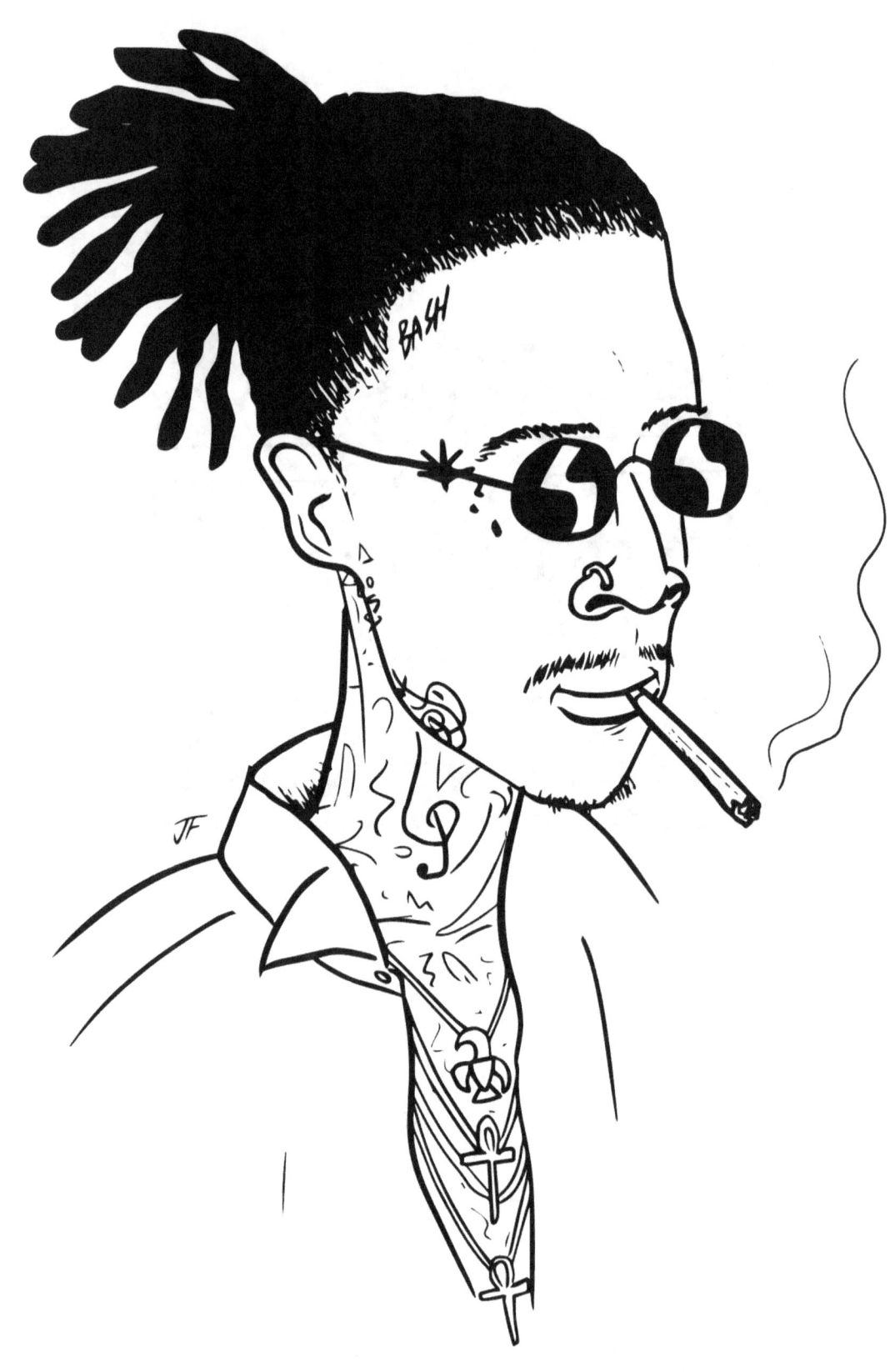

Wiz Khalifa

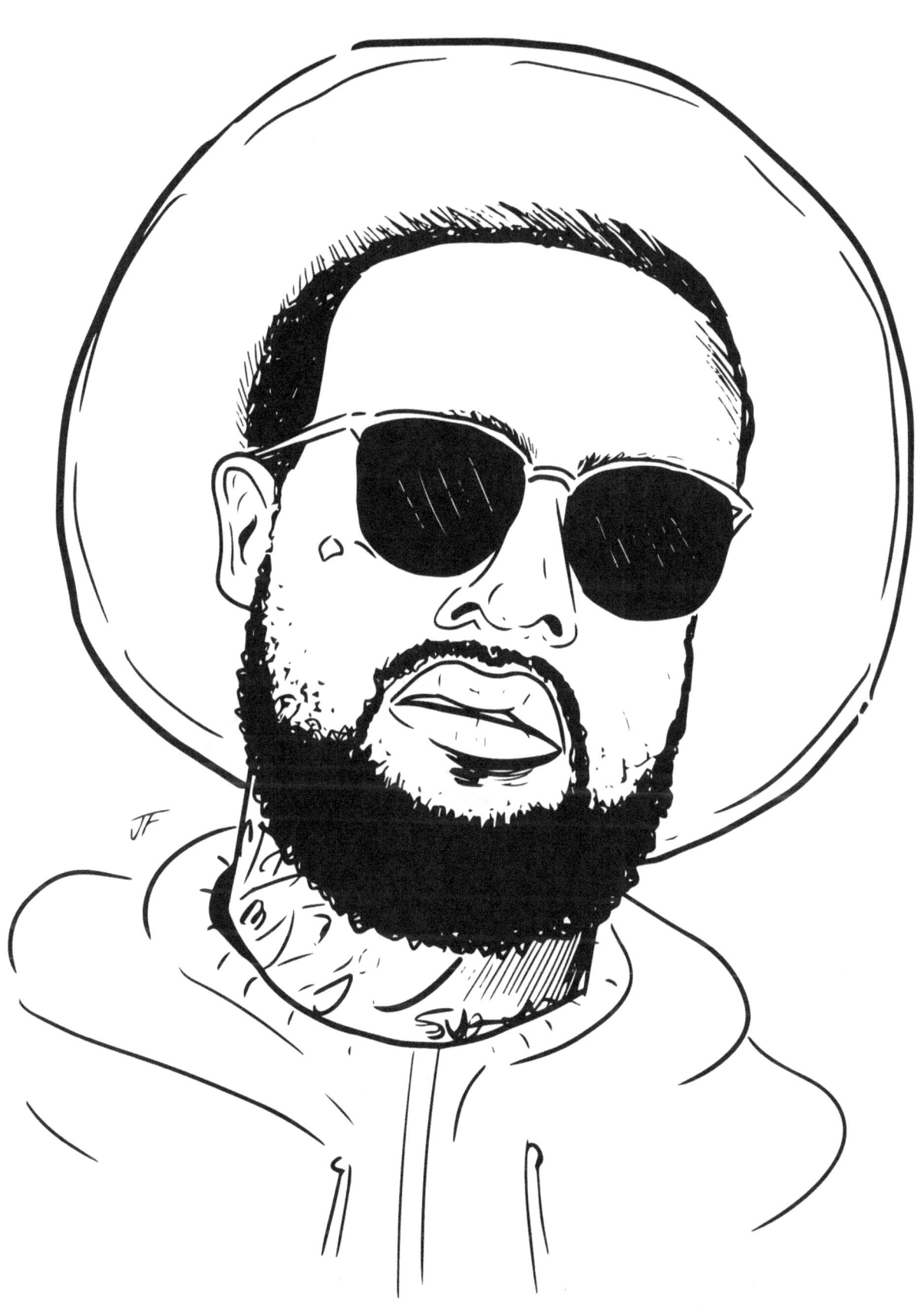

ScHoolboy Q

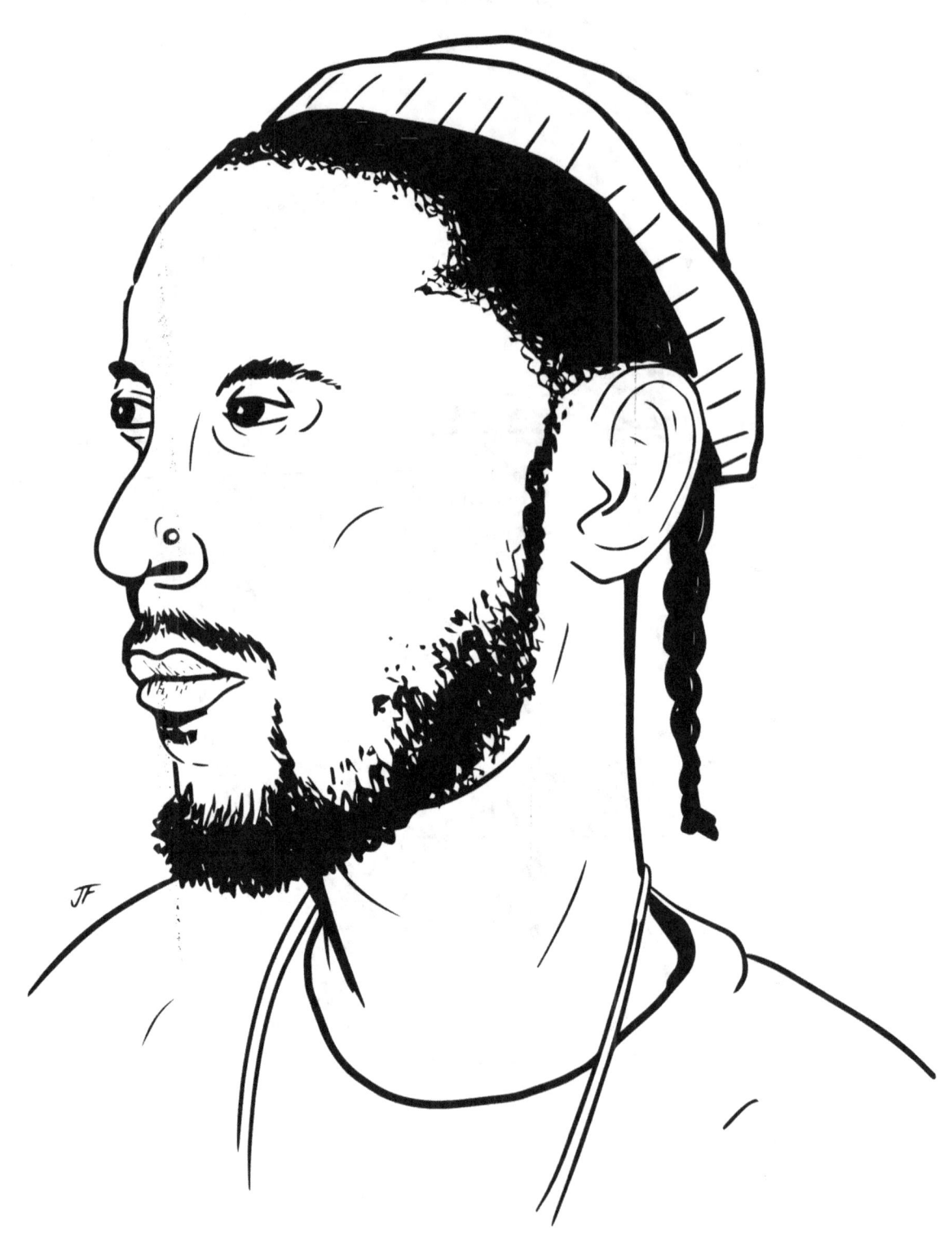

Kendrick Lamar

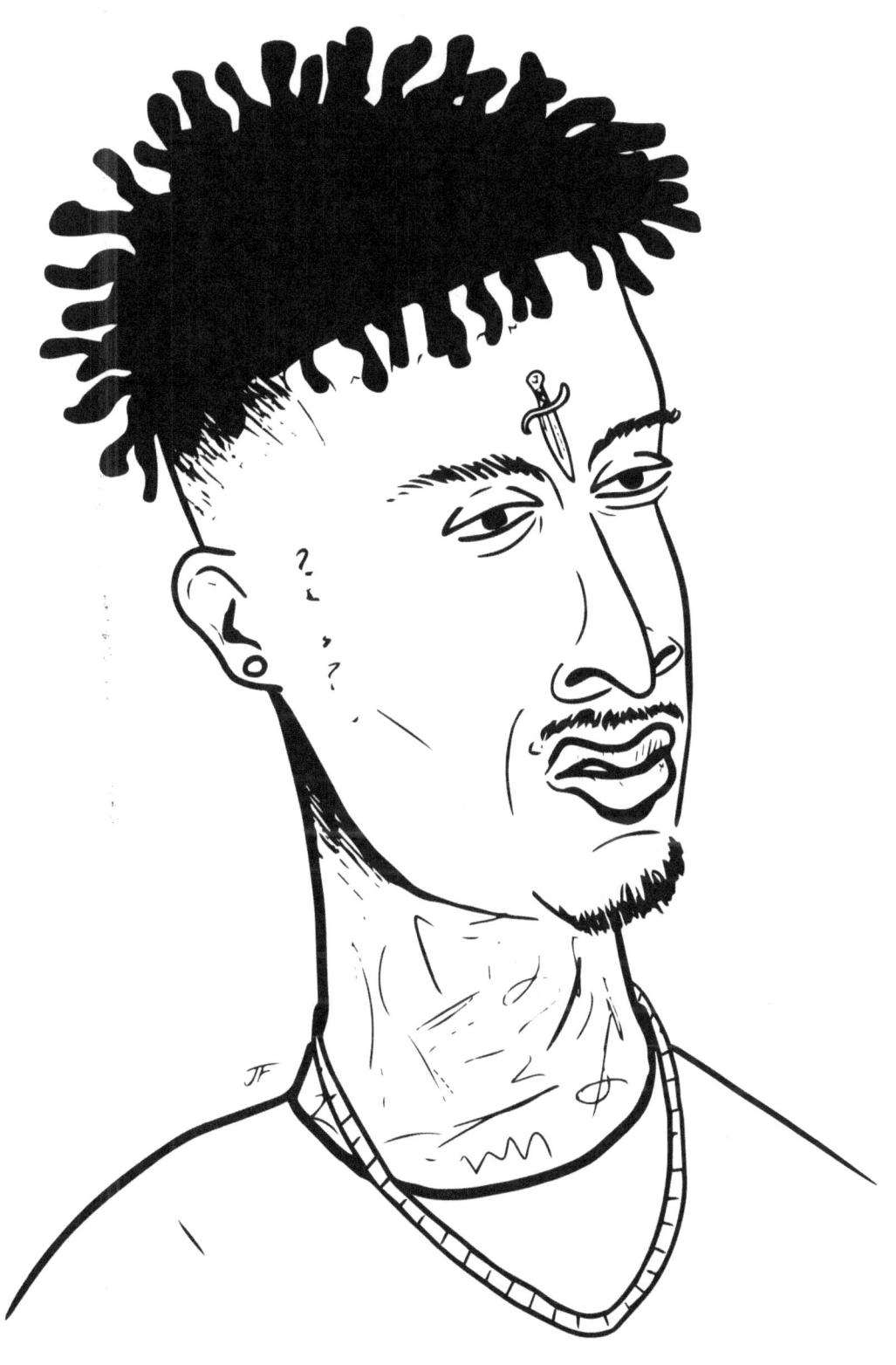

21 Savage

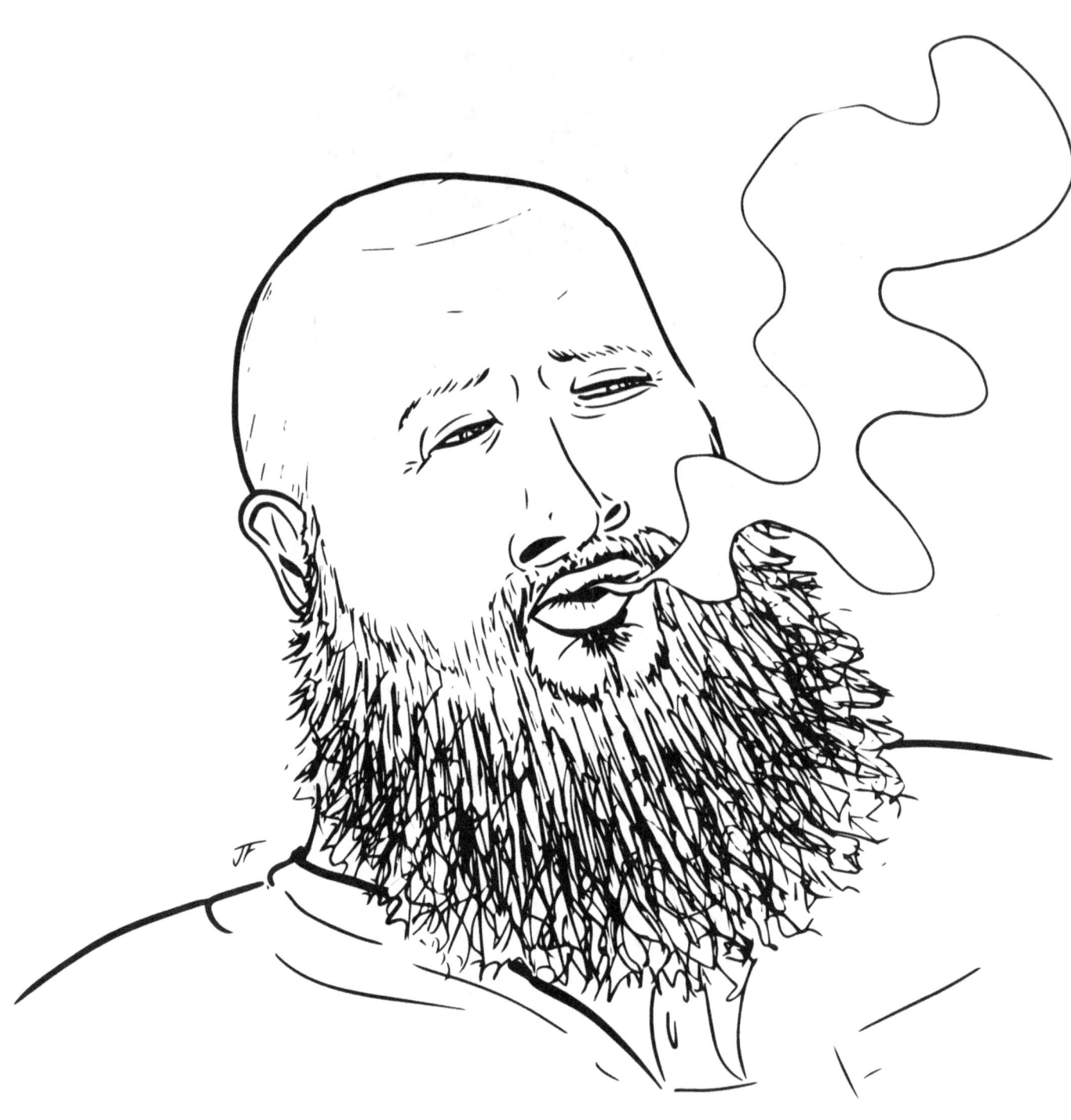

Action Bronson

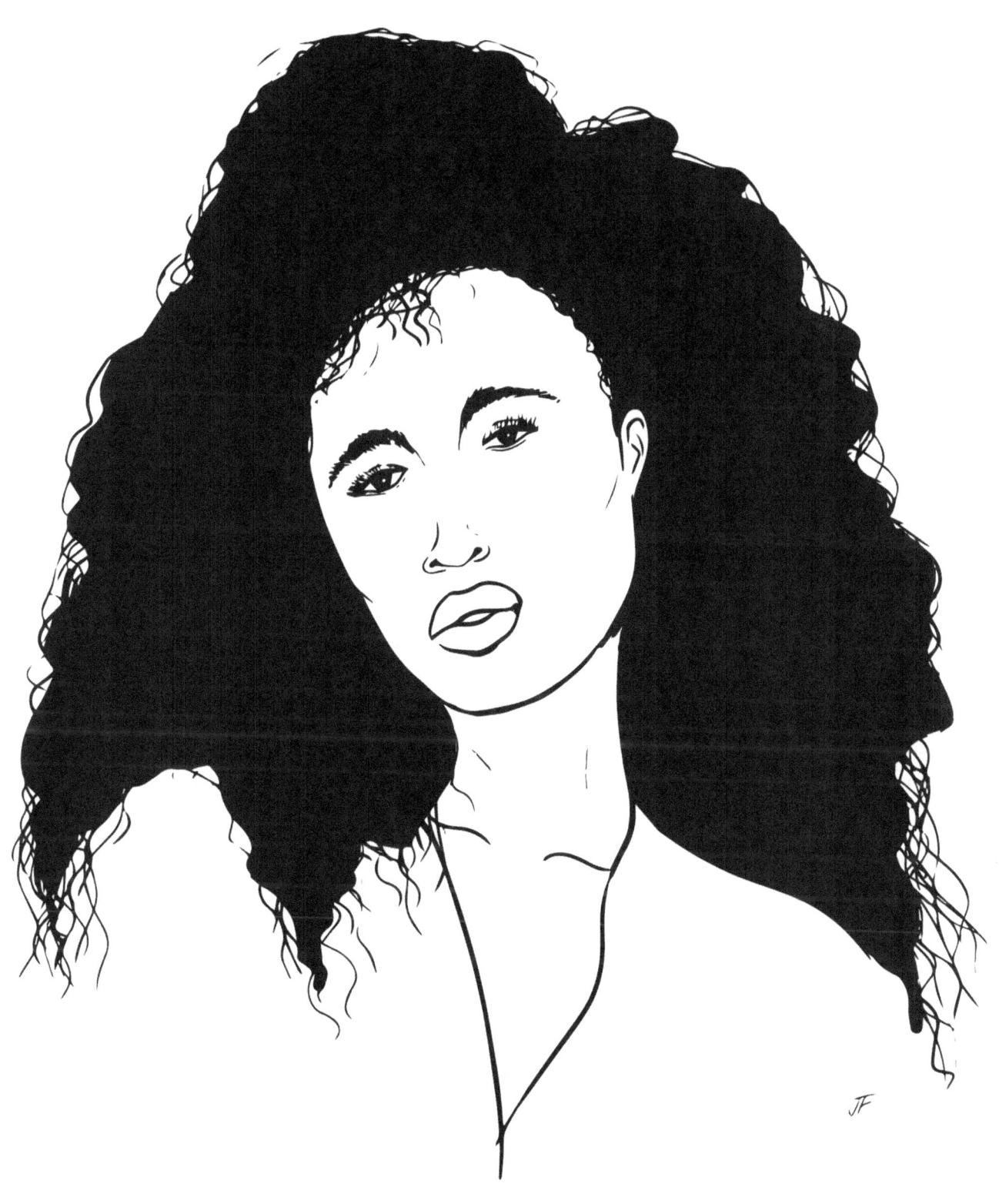

SZA

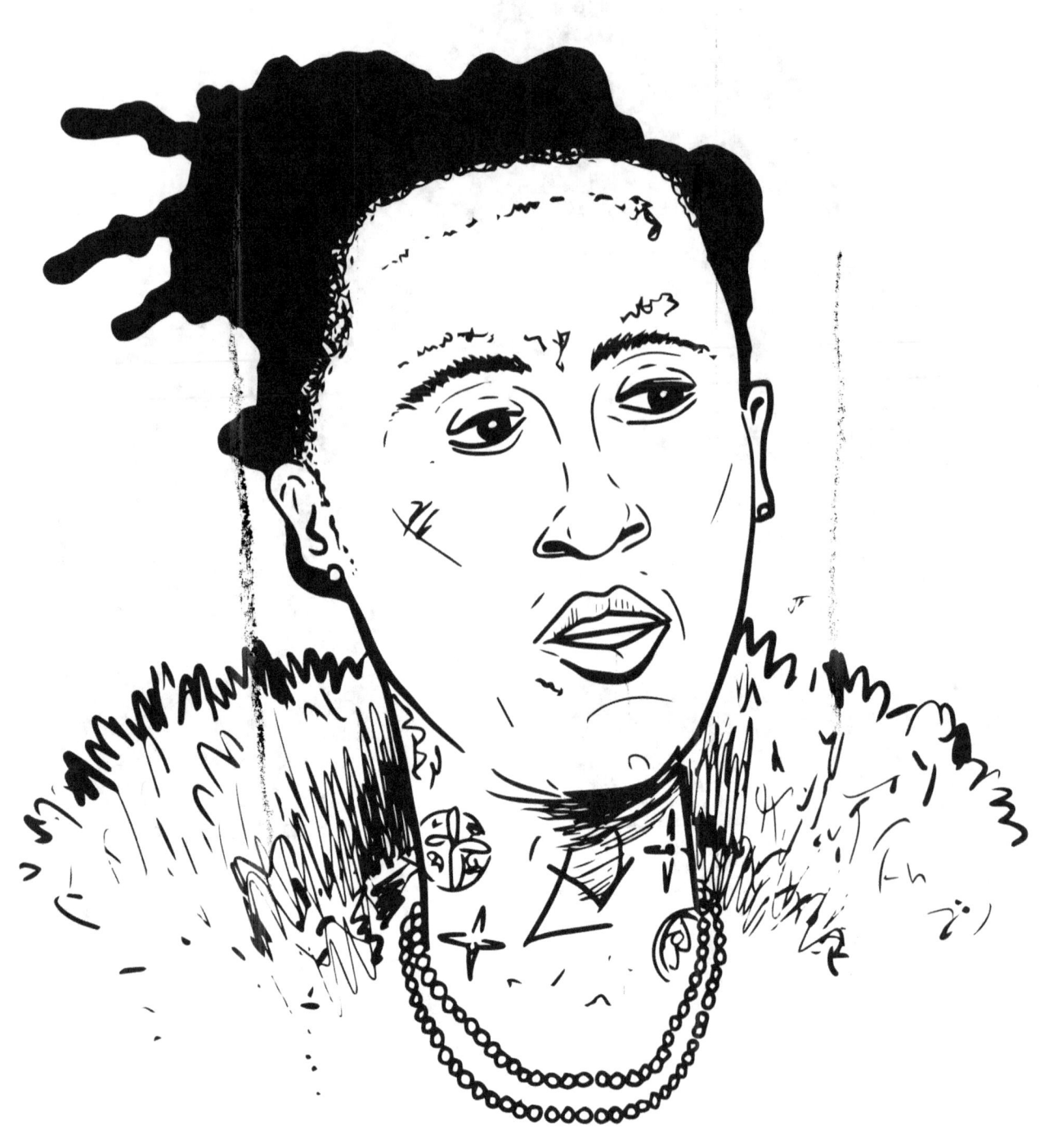

Young Thug

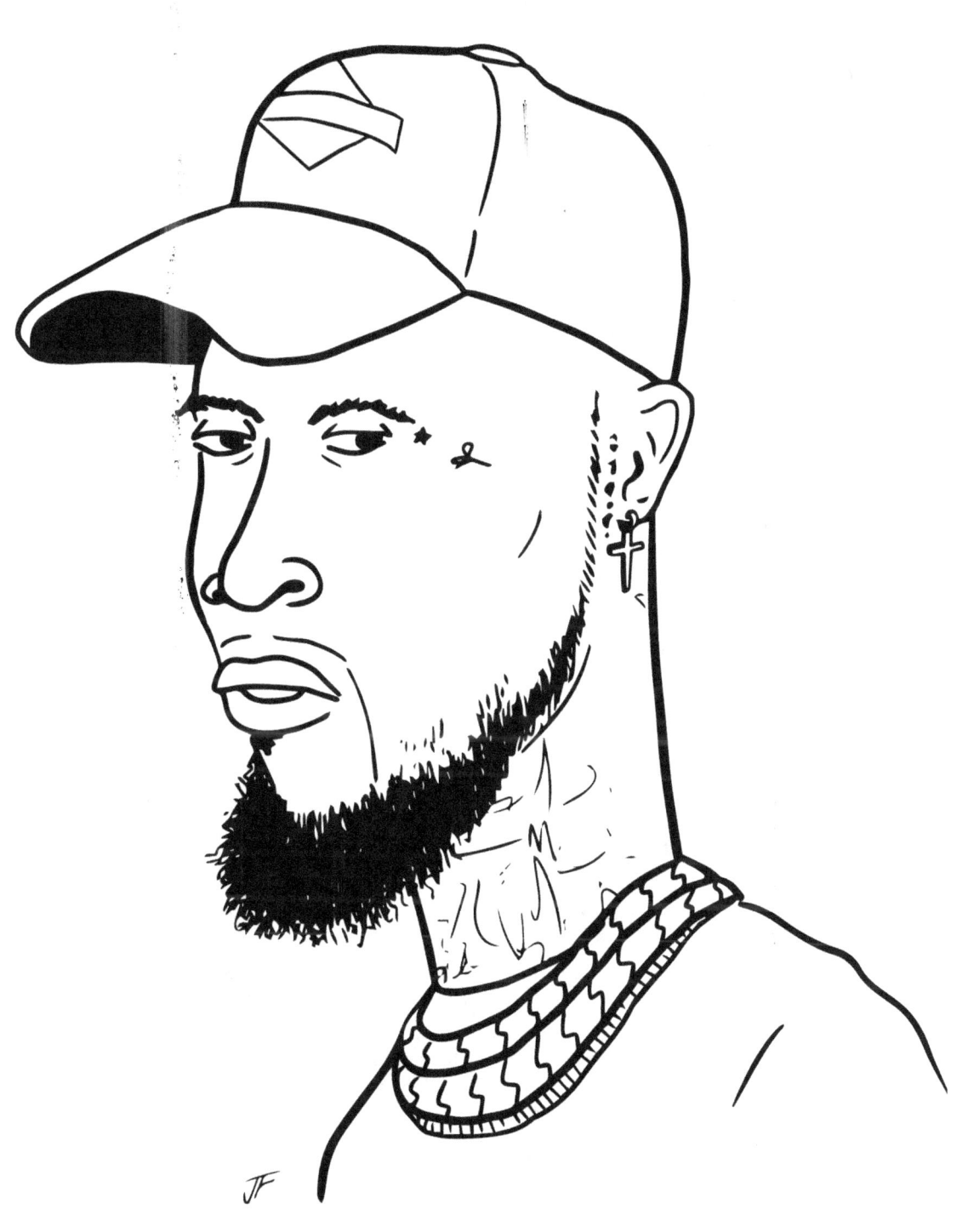

Tory Lanez

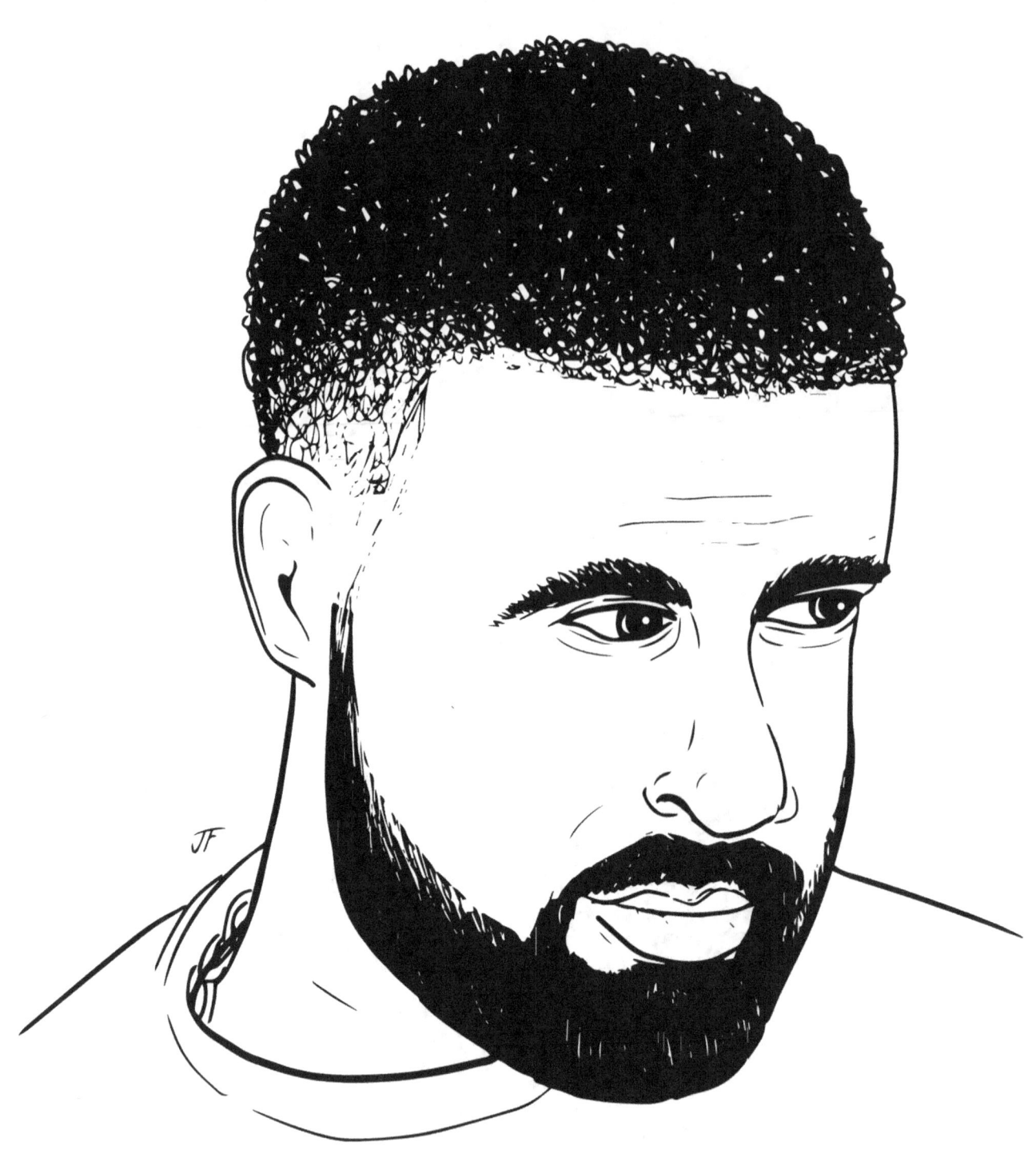

Drake

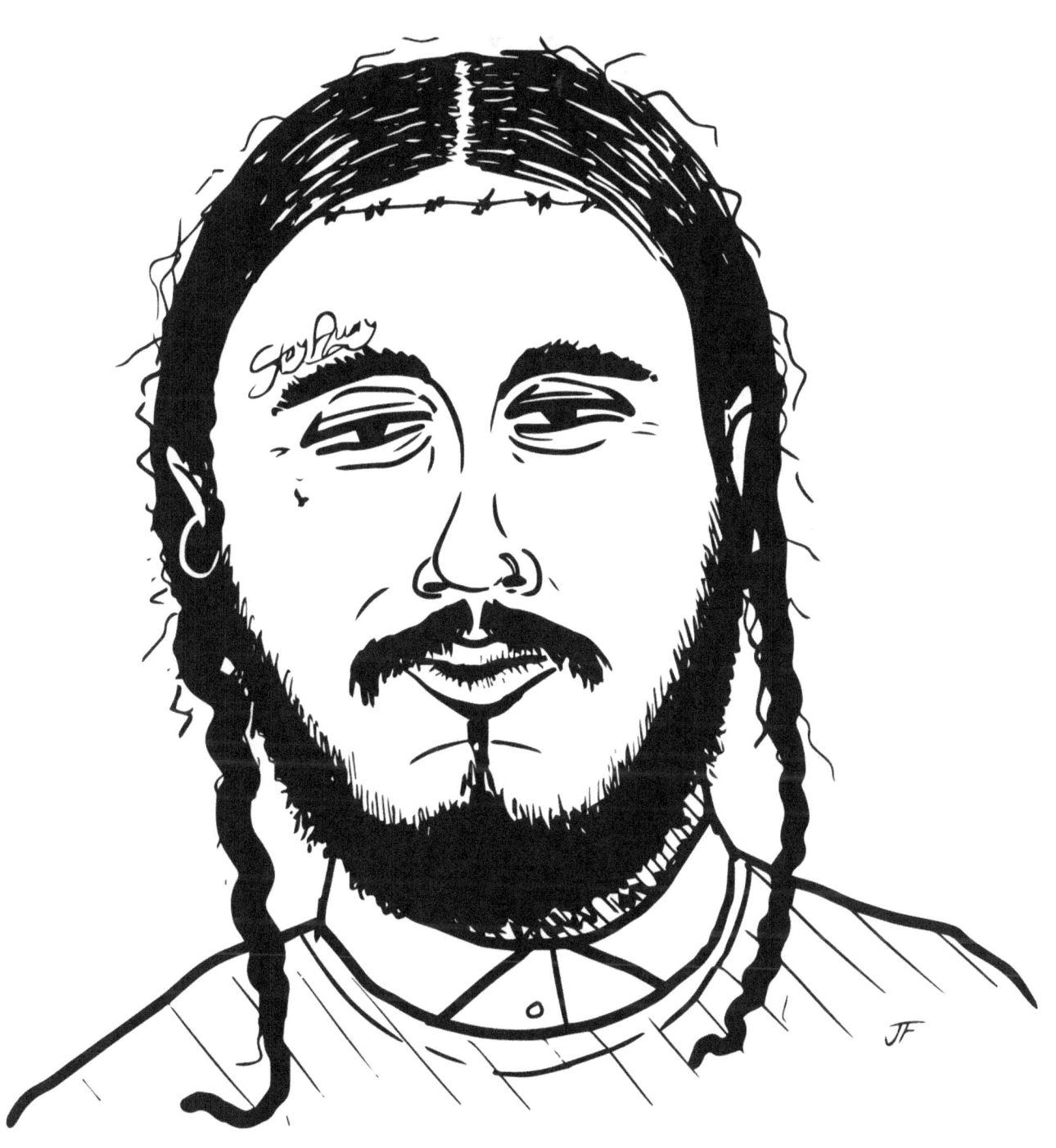

Post Malone

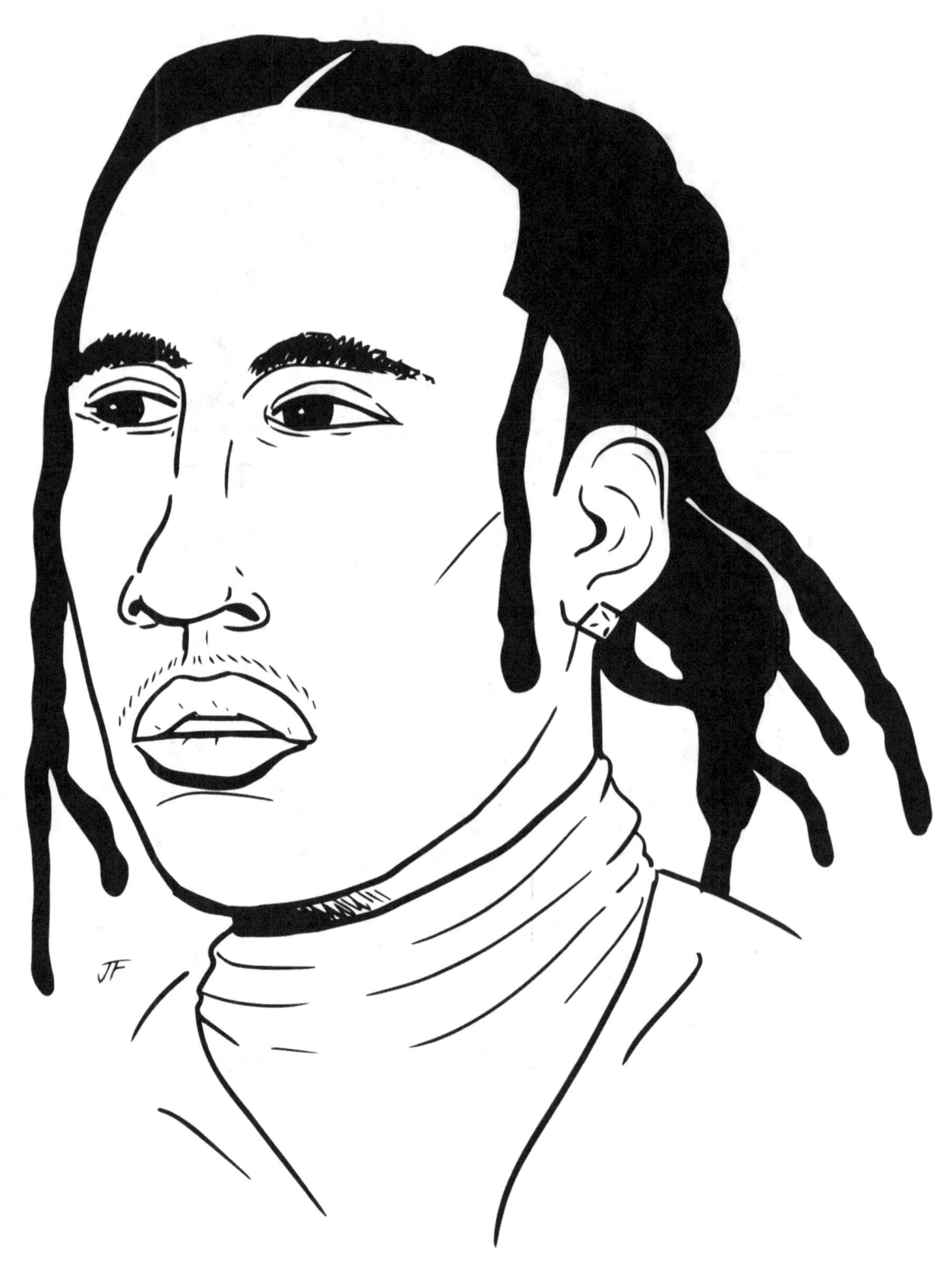

A$AP Rocky

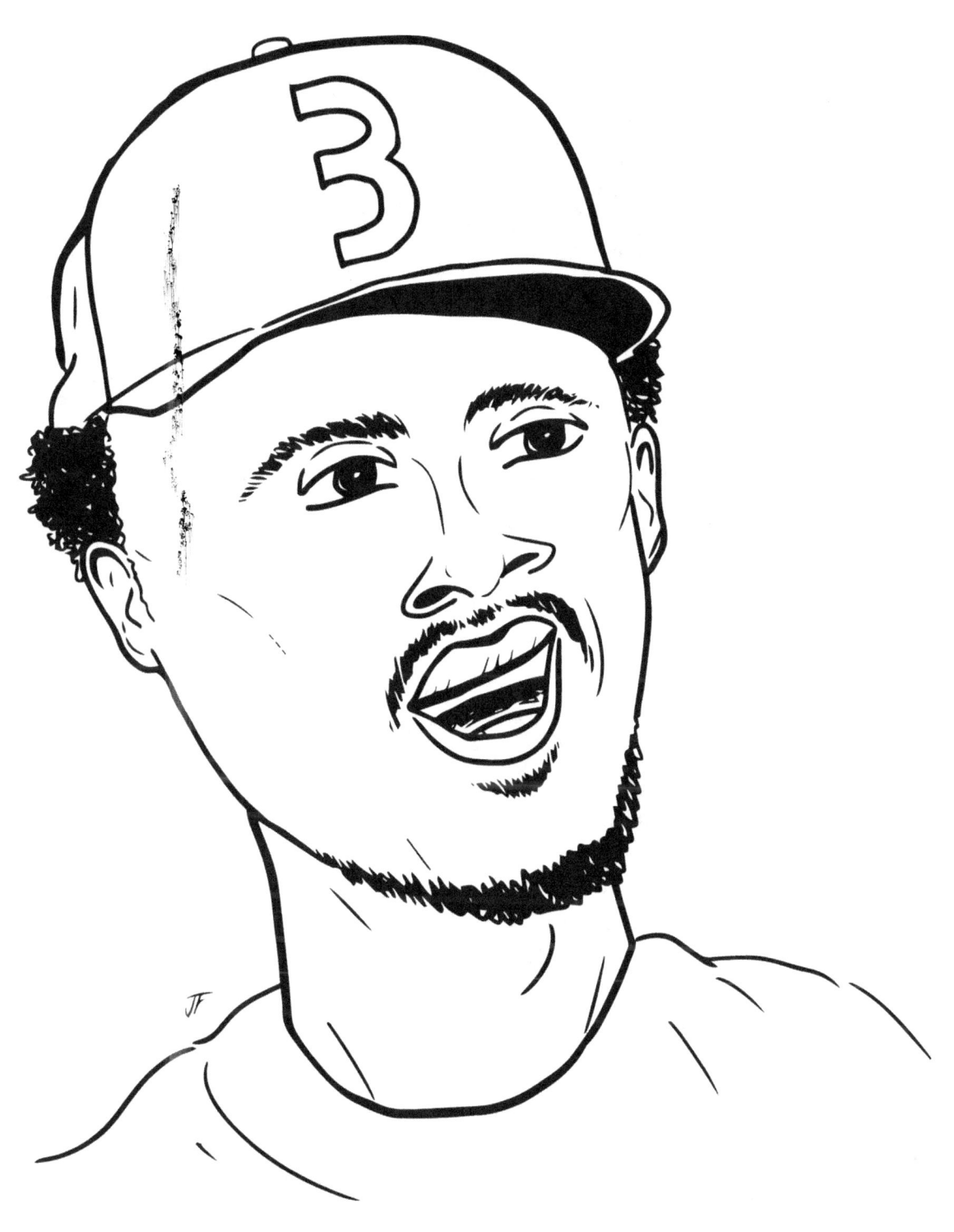

Chance the Rapper

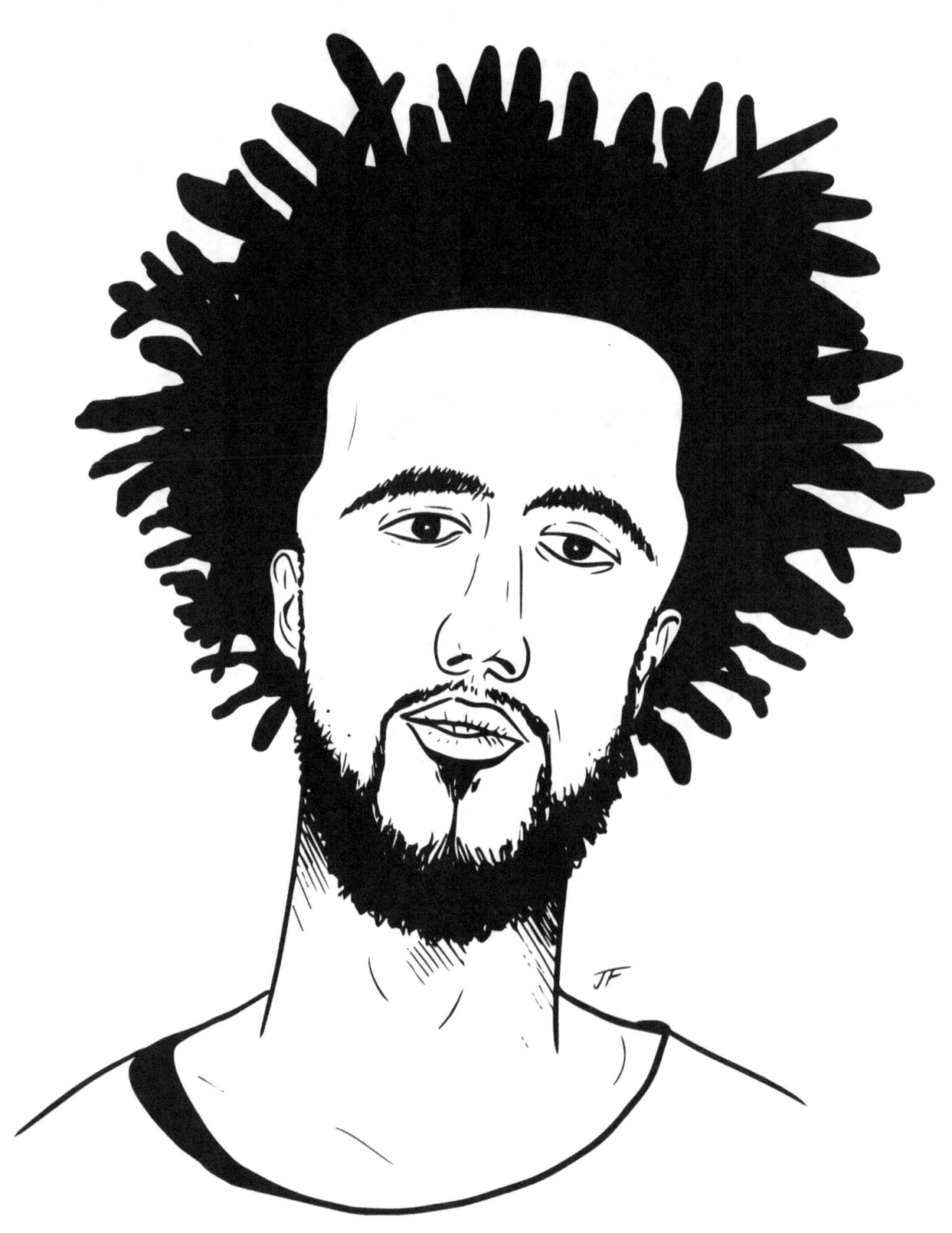

J. Cole

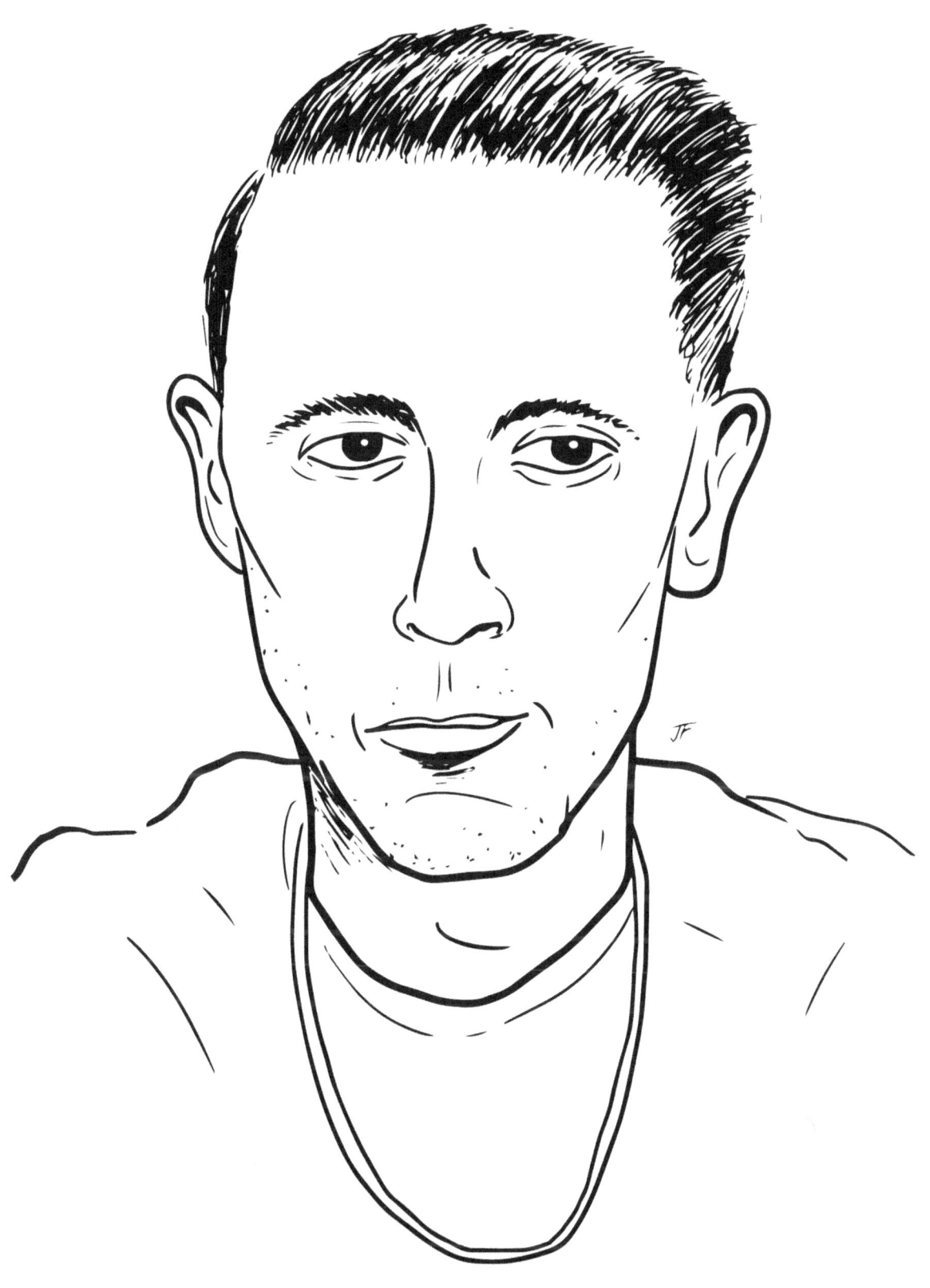

G-Eazy

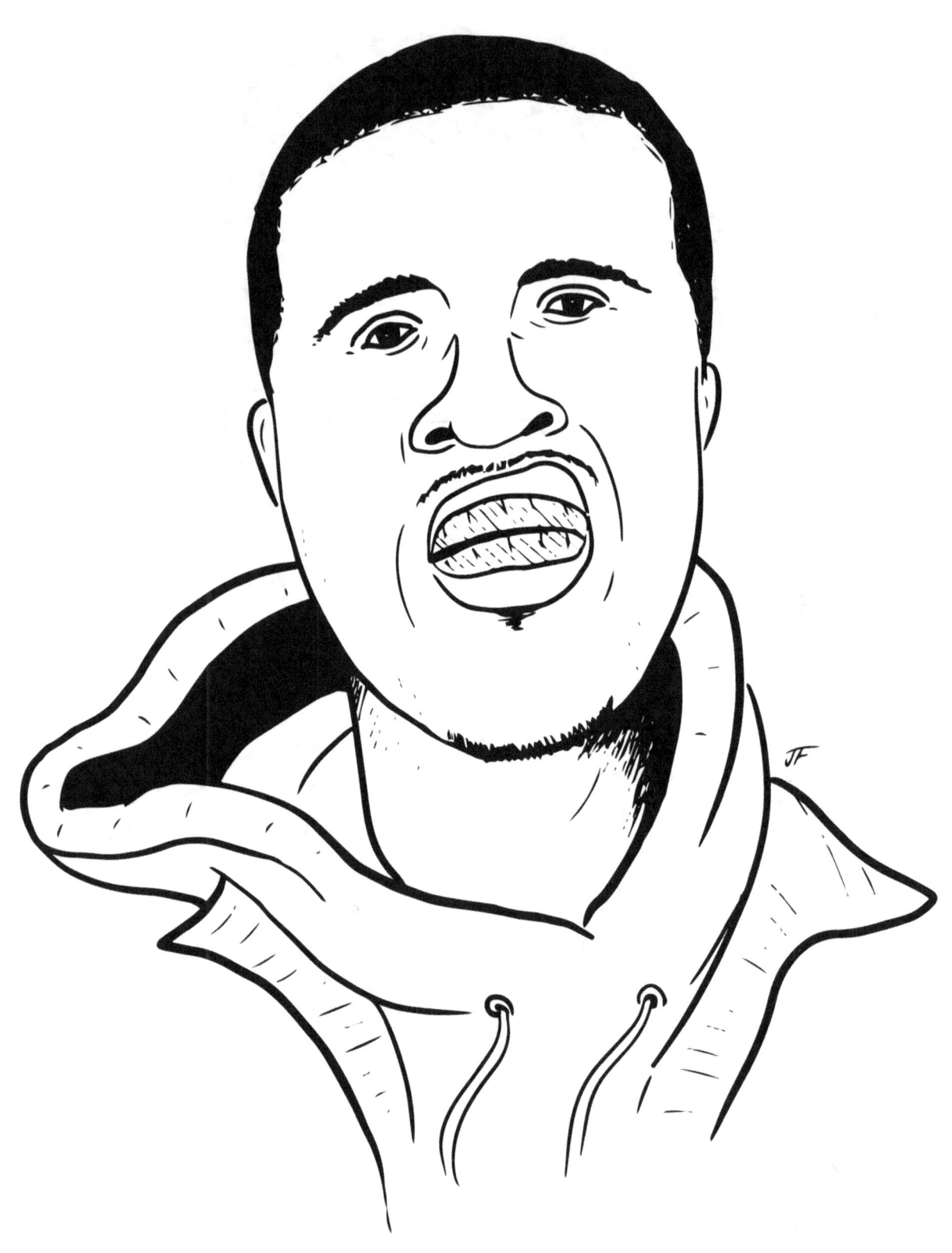

A$AP Ferg

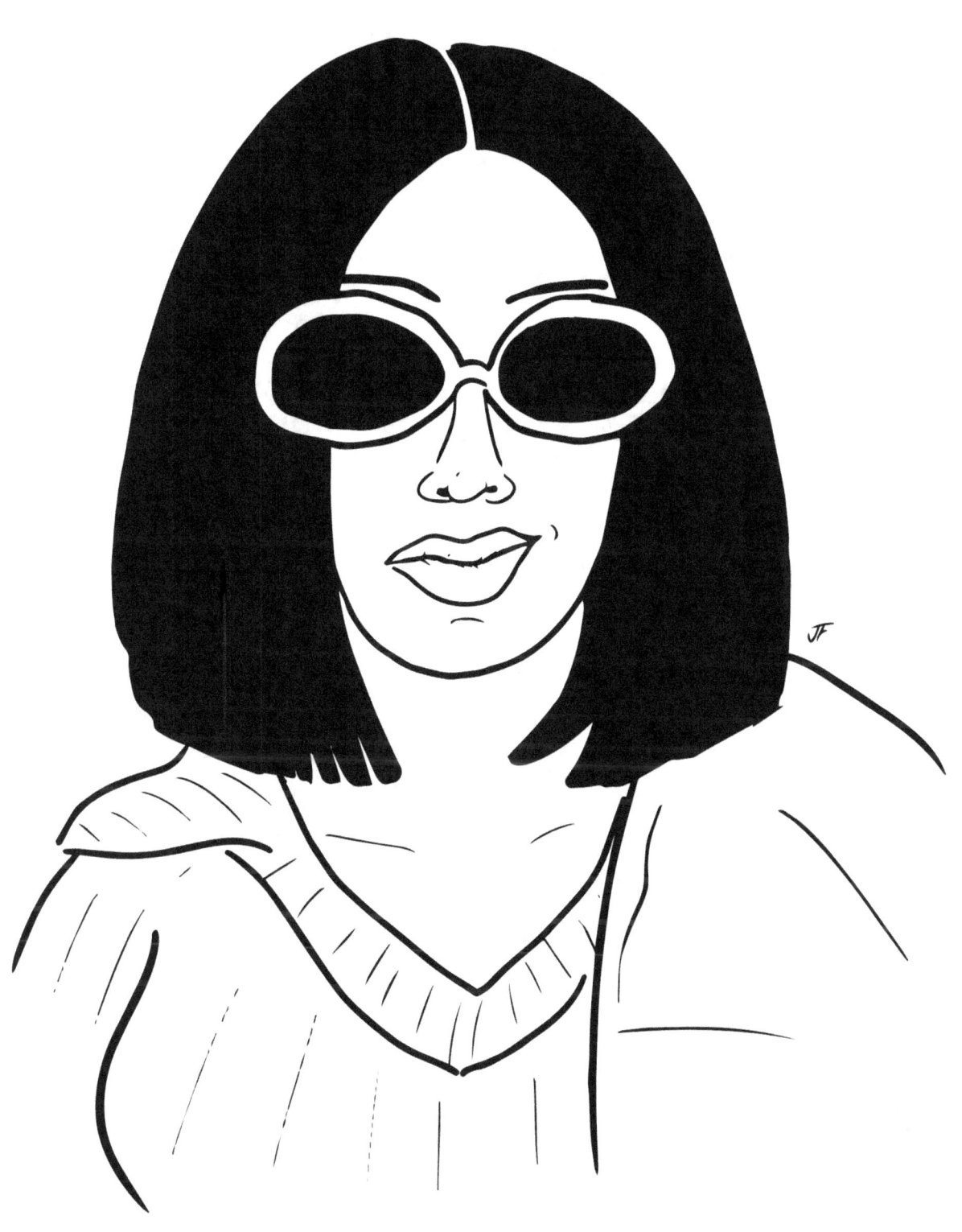

Cardi B

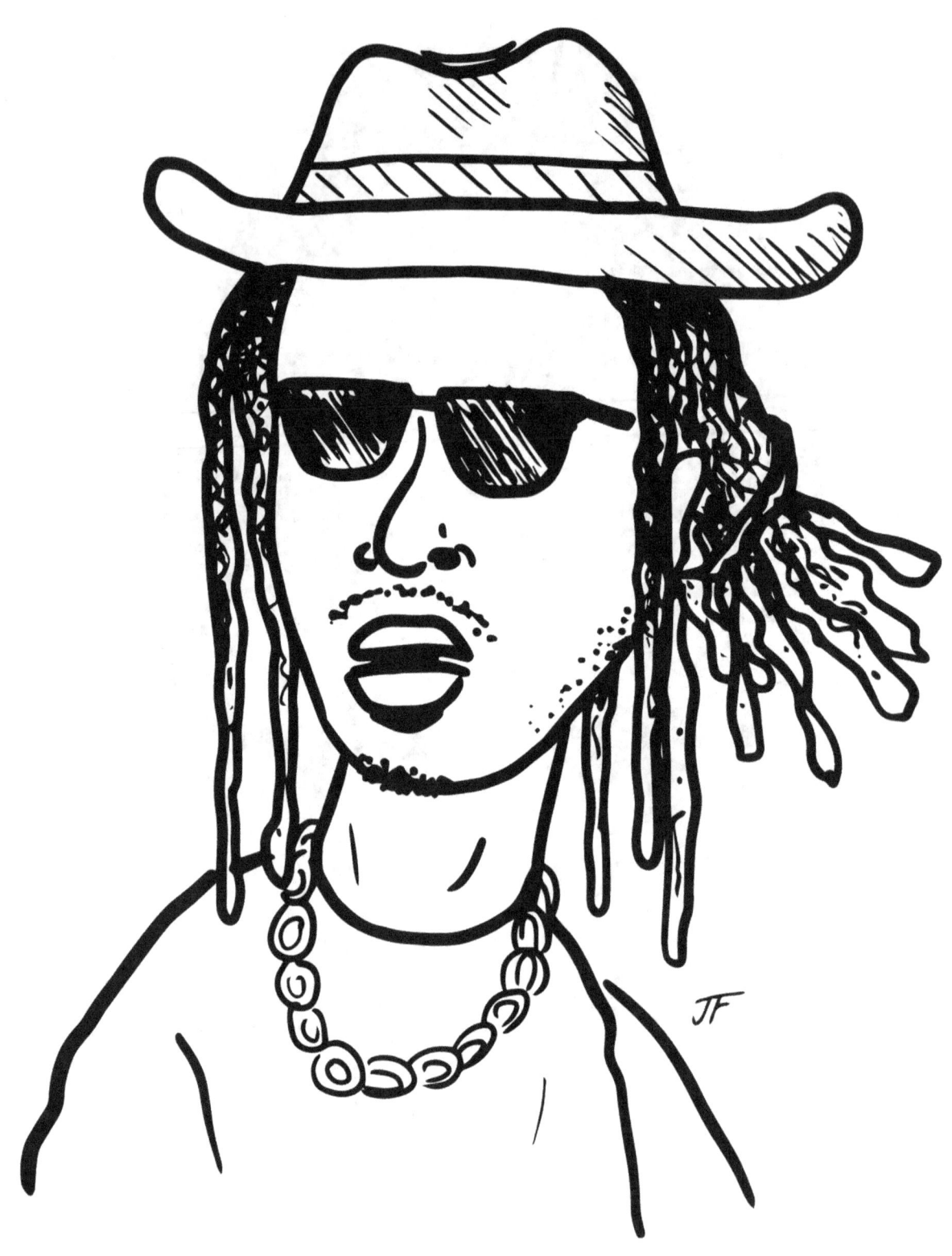

Future

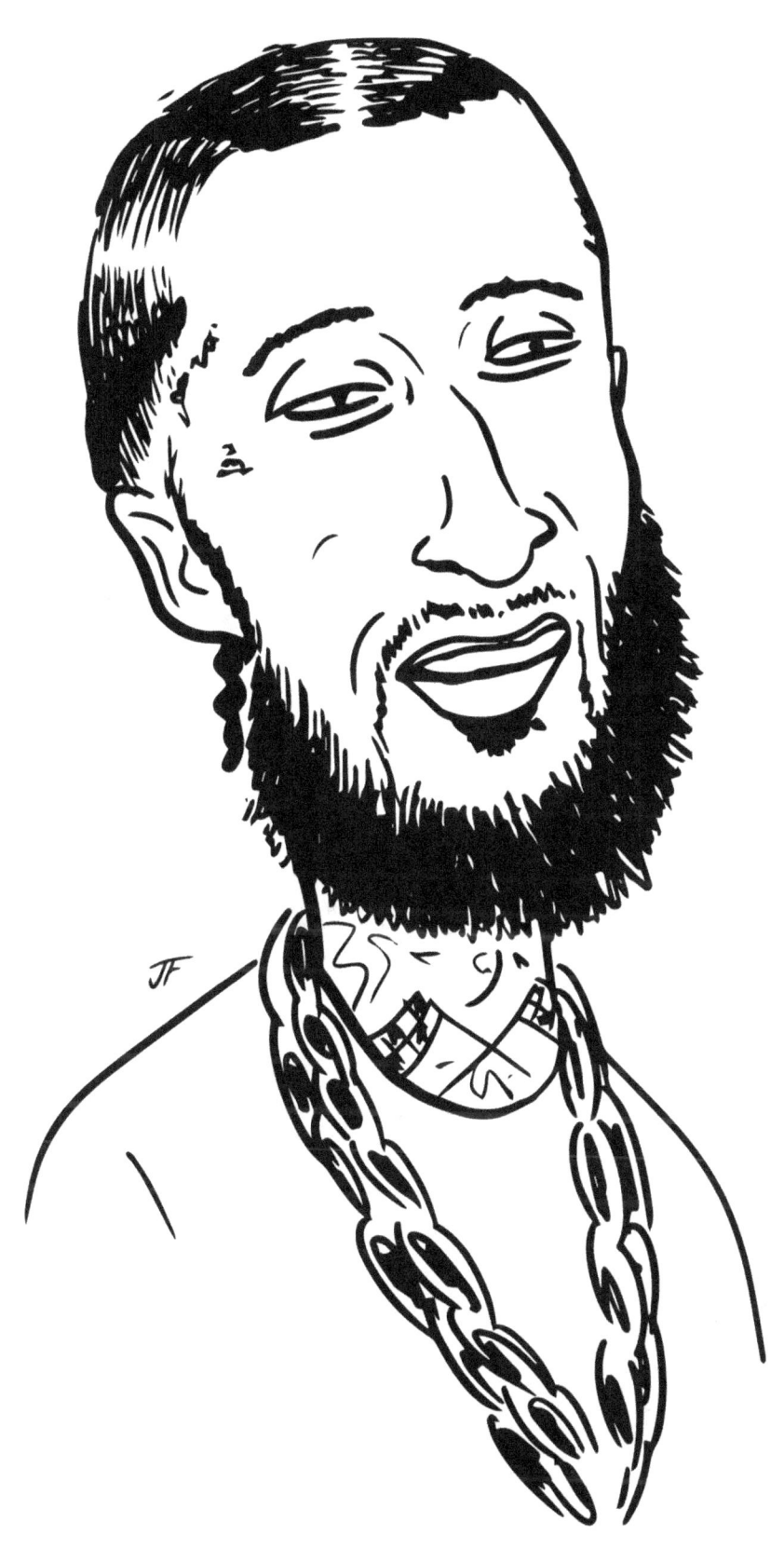

Nipsey Hussle

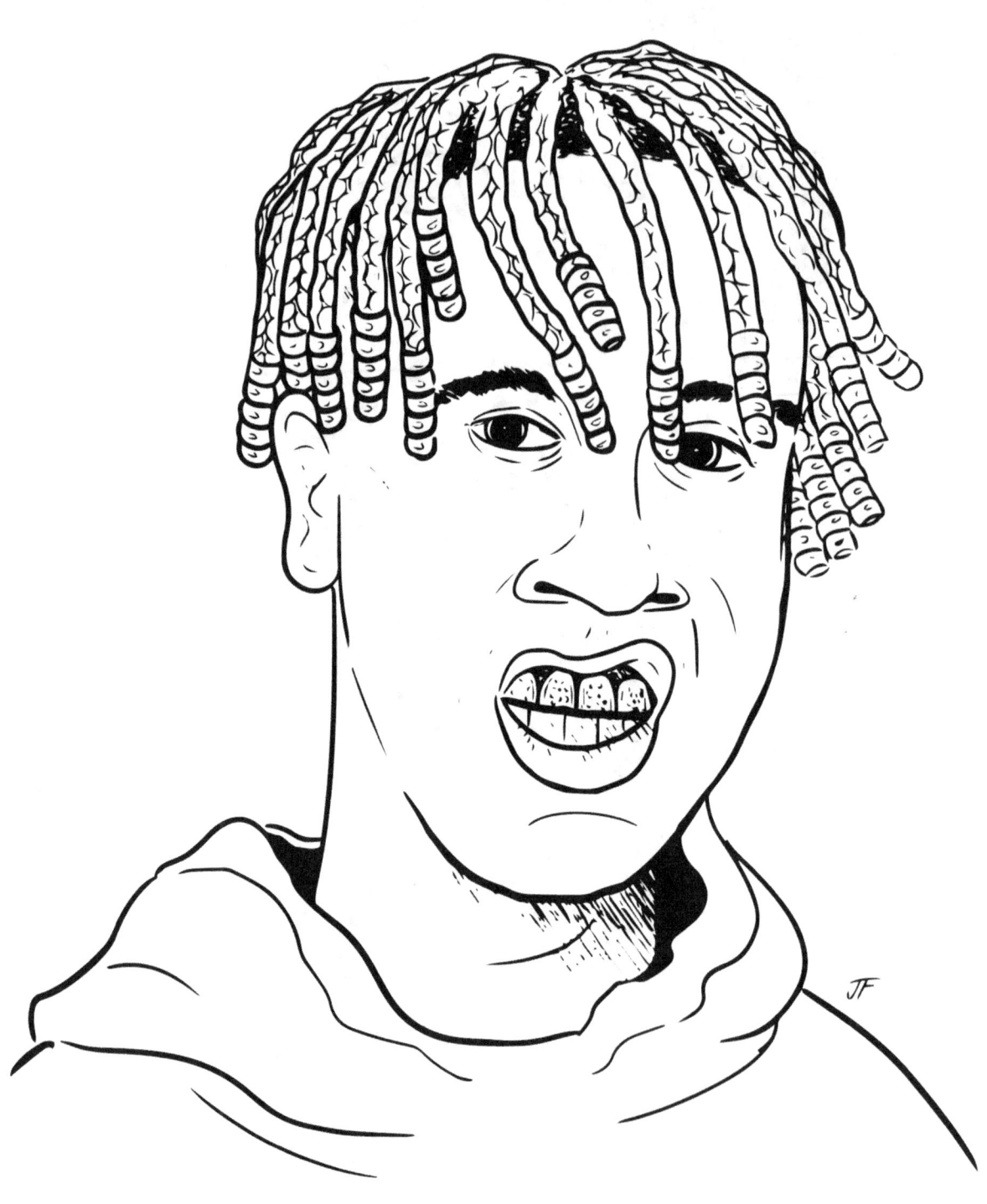

Lil' Yachty

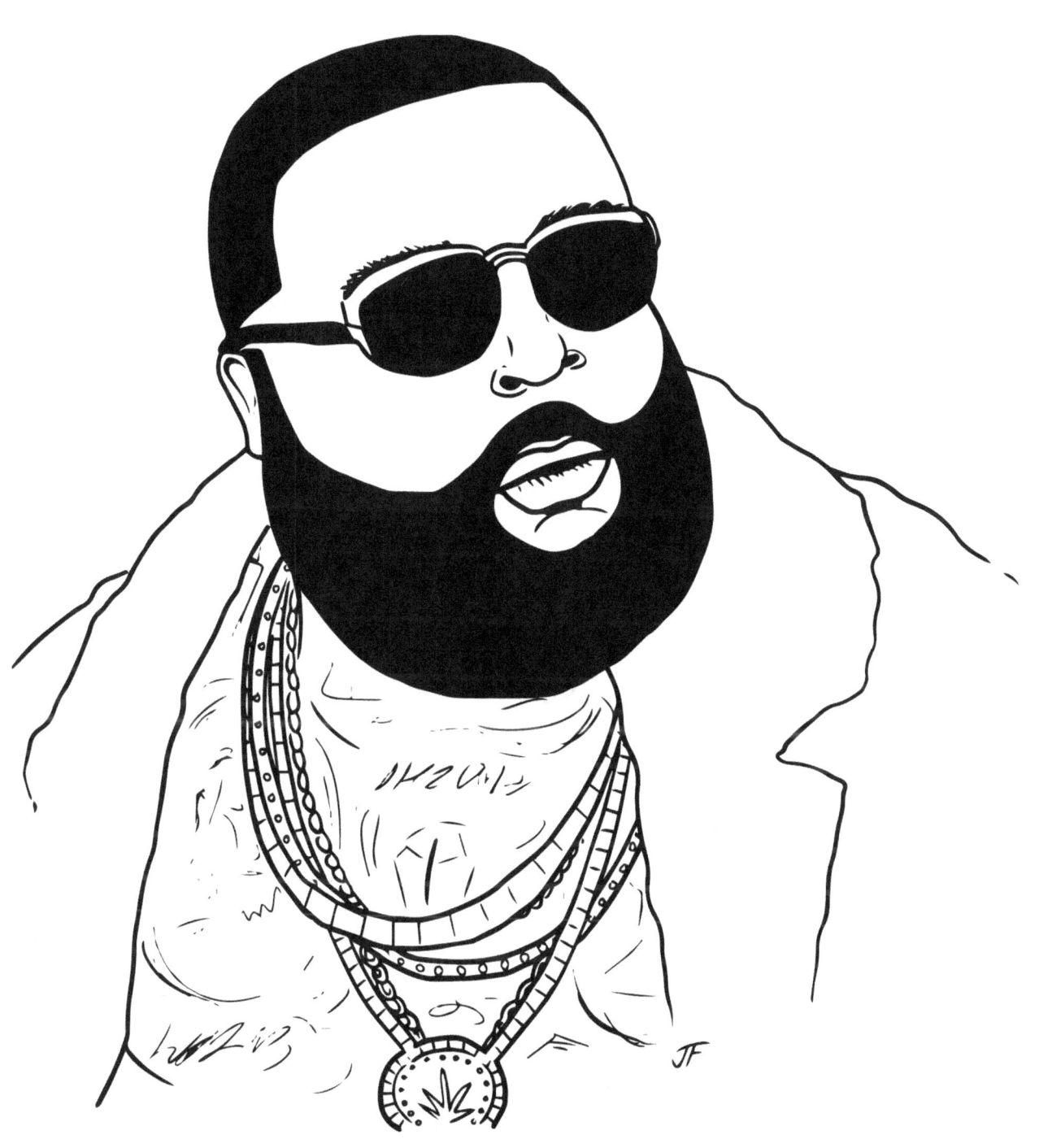

Rick Ross

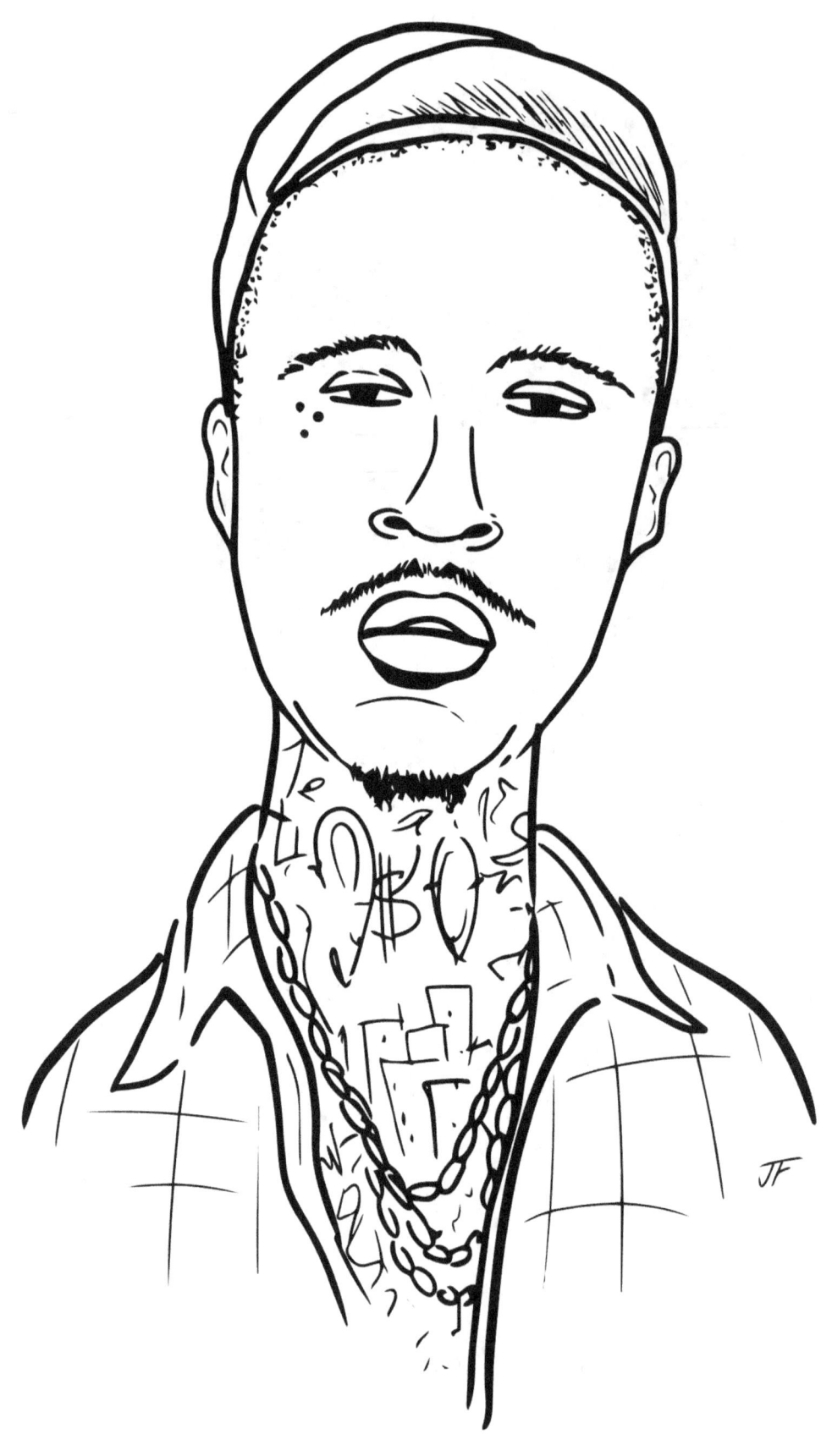

YG

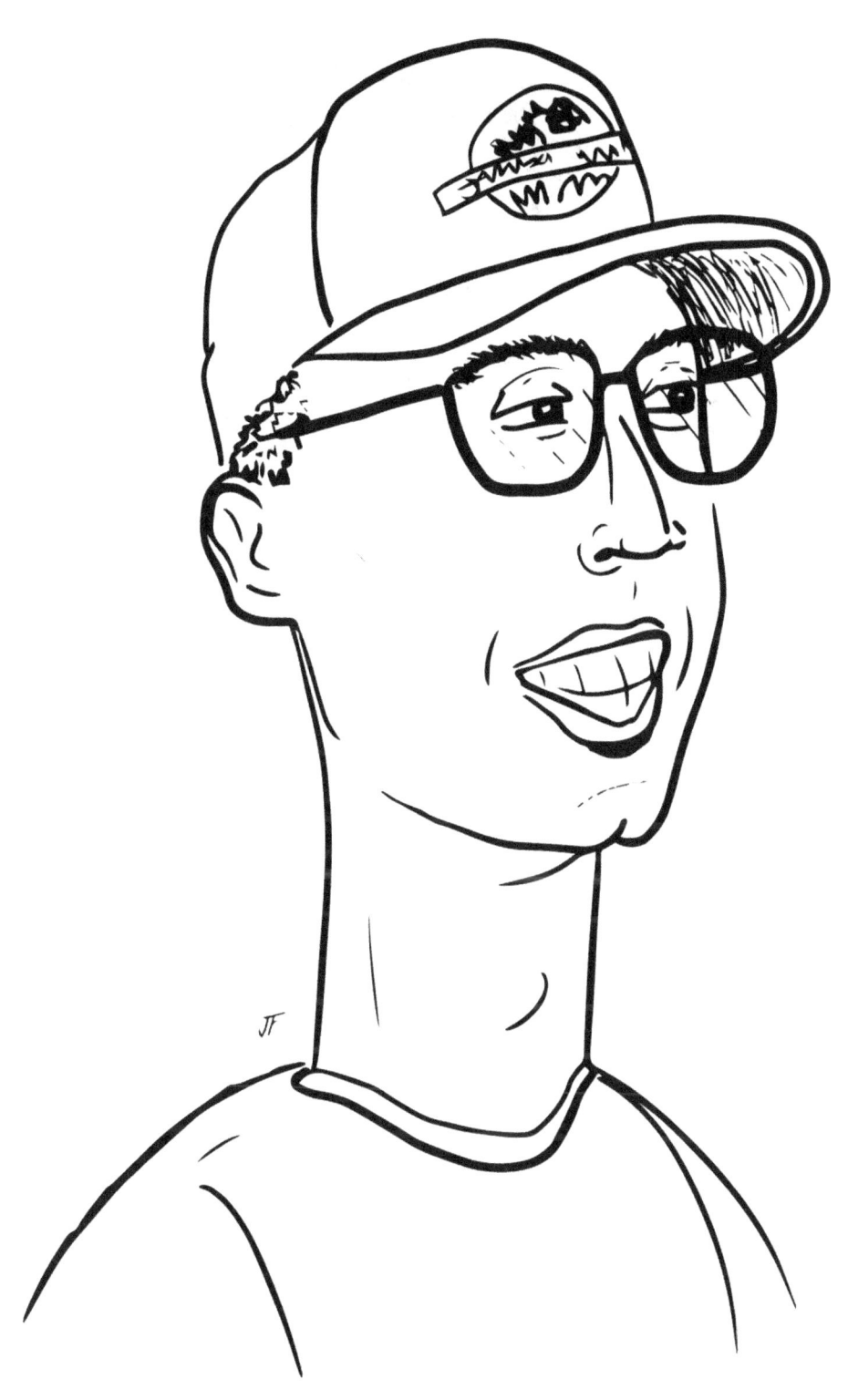

Logic

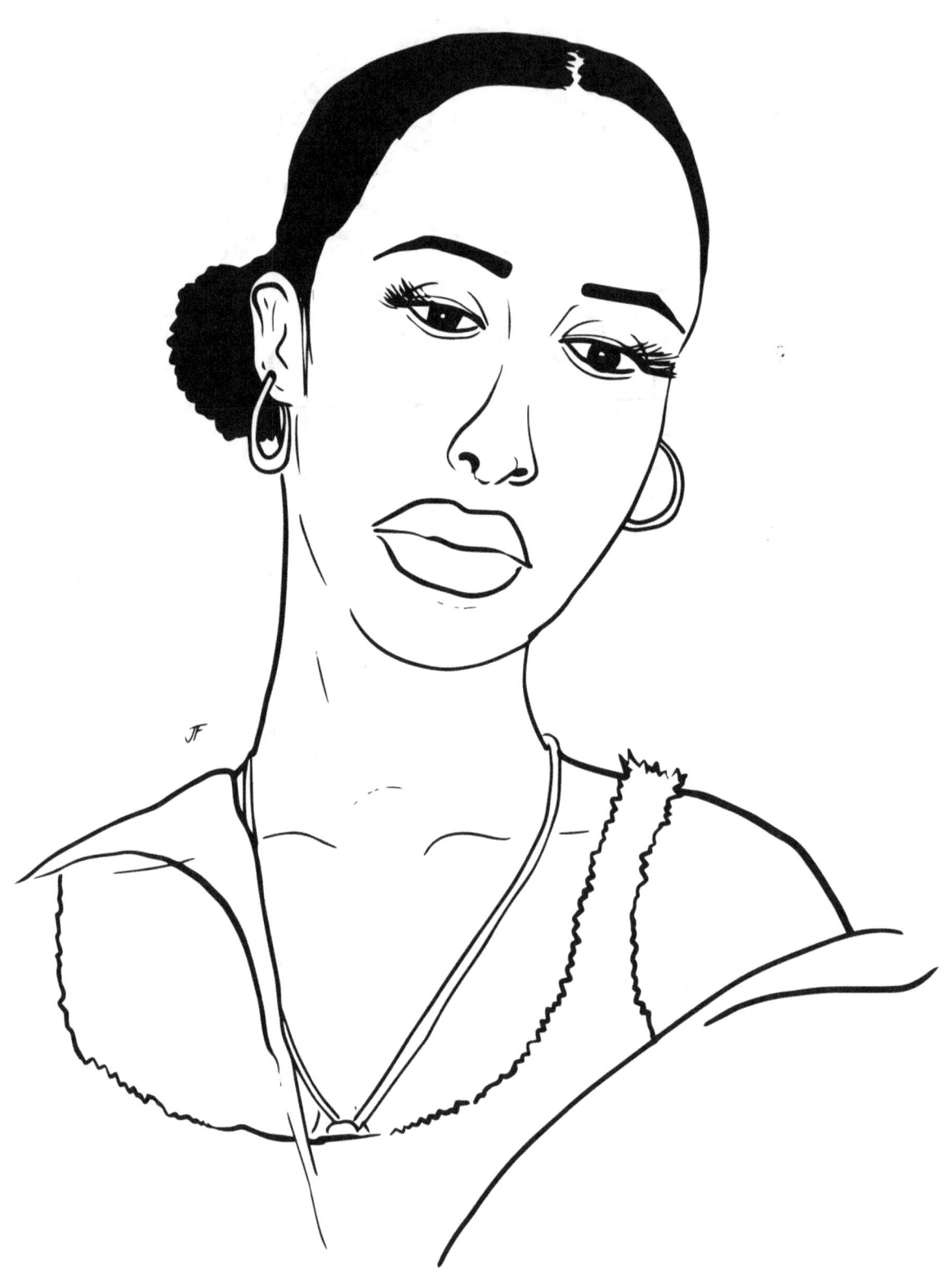

Jorja Smith

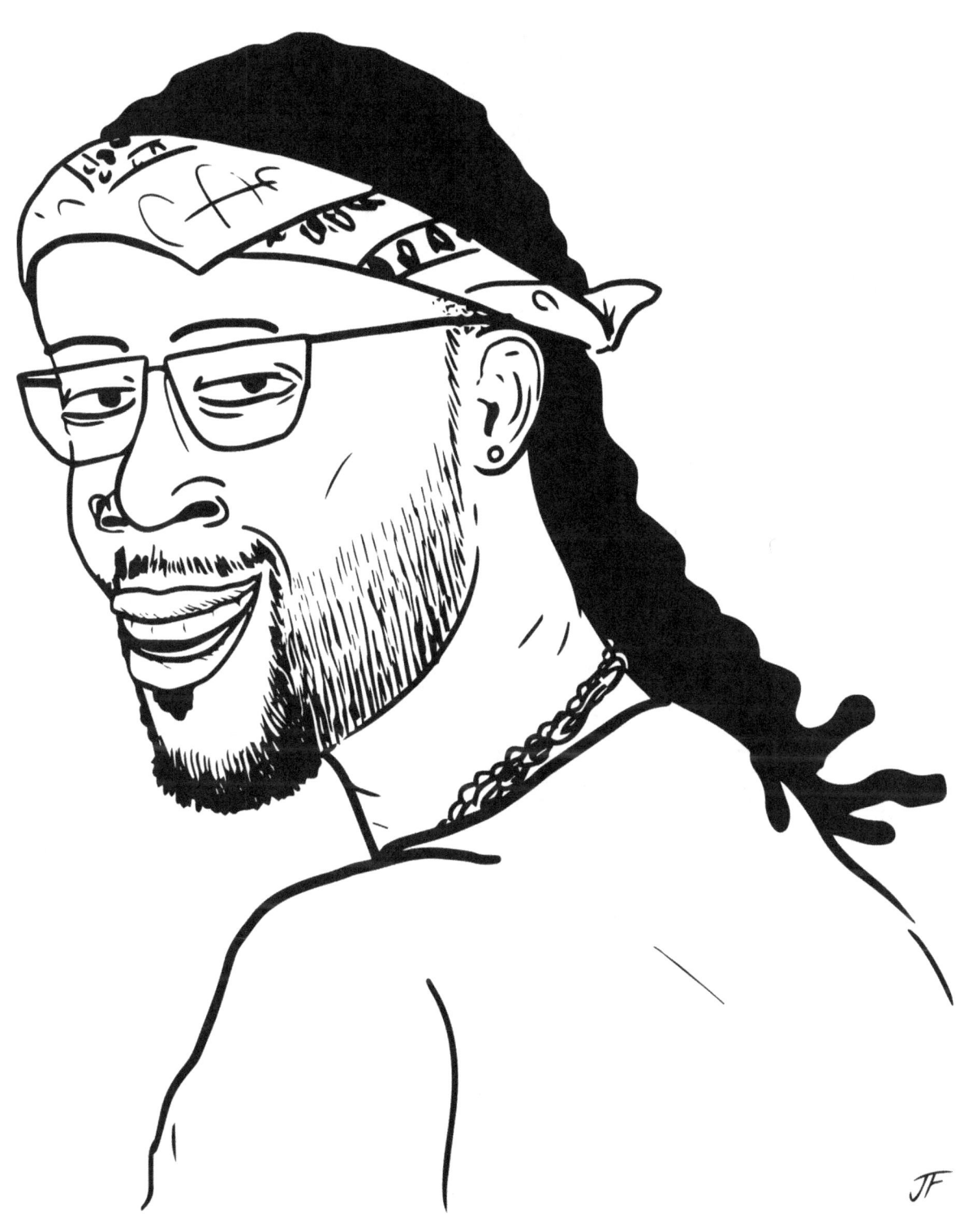

PartyNextDoor

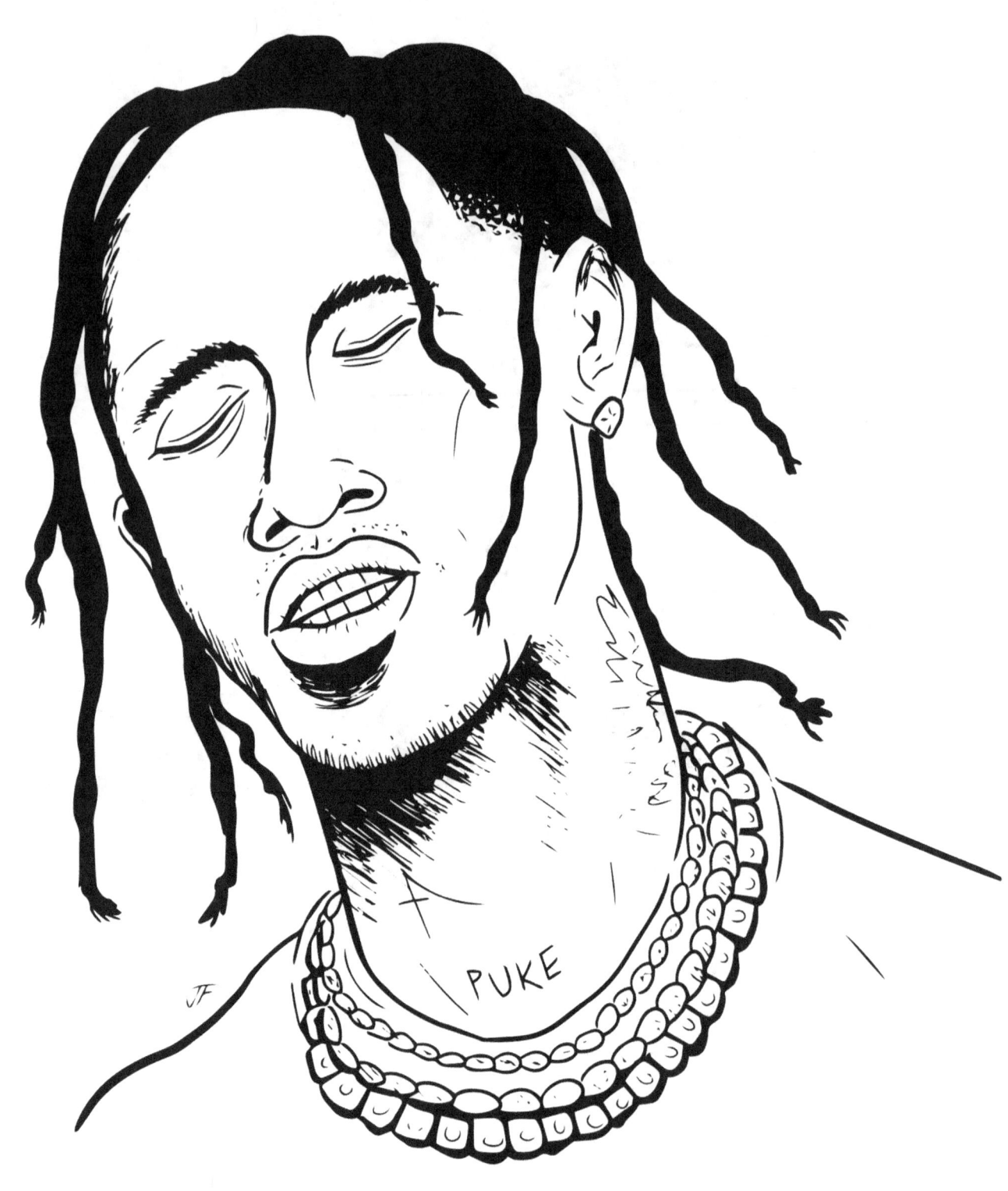

Travis Scott

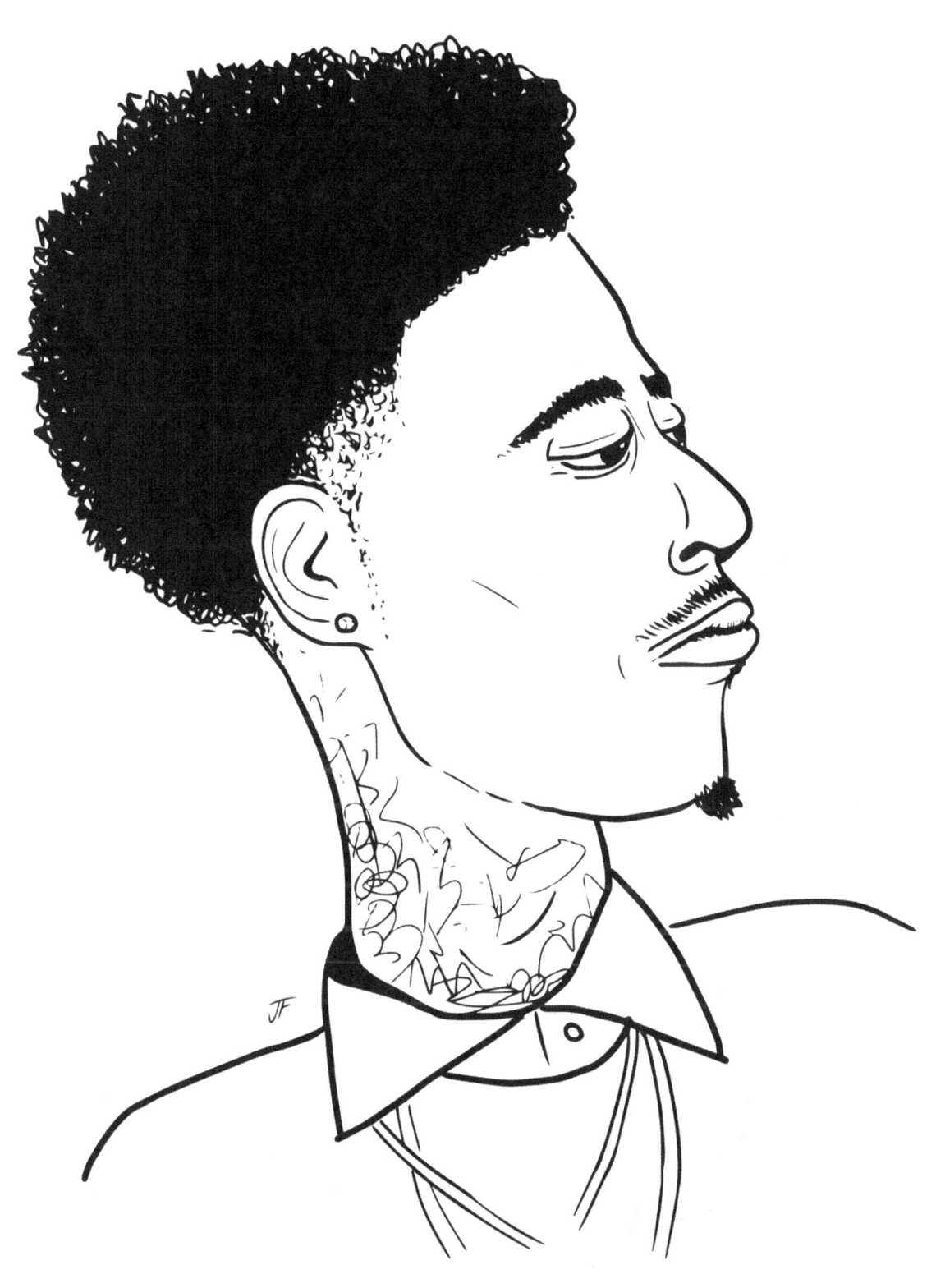

Rich Homie Quan

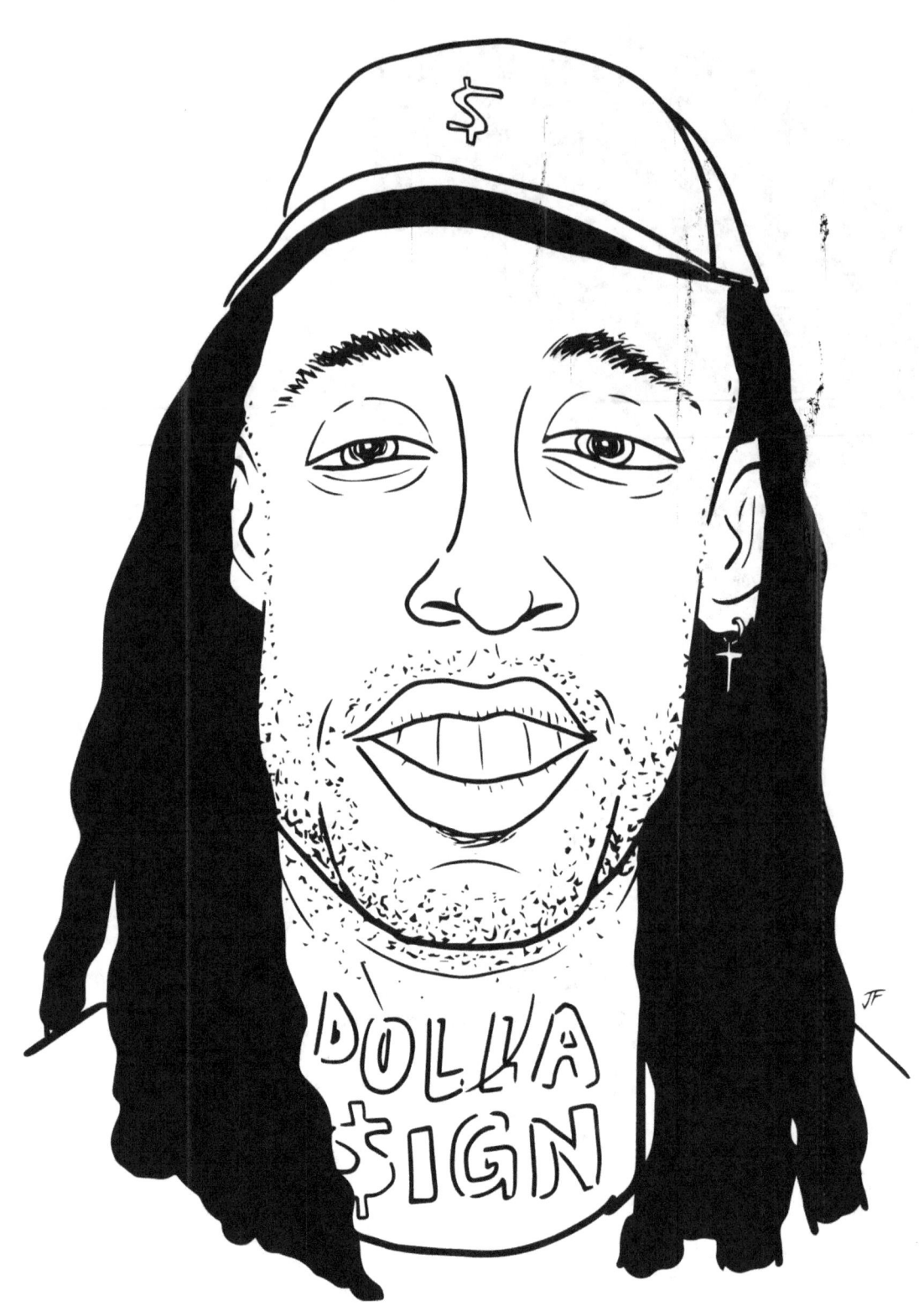

Ty Dolla $ign

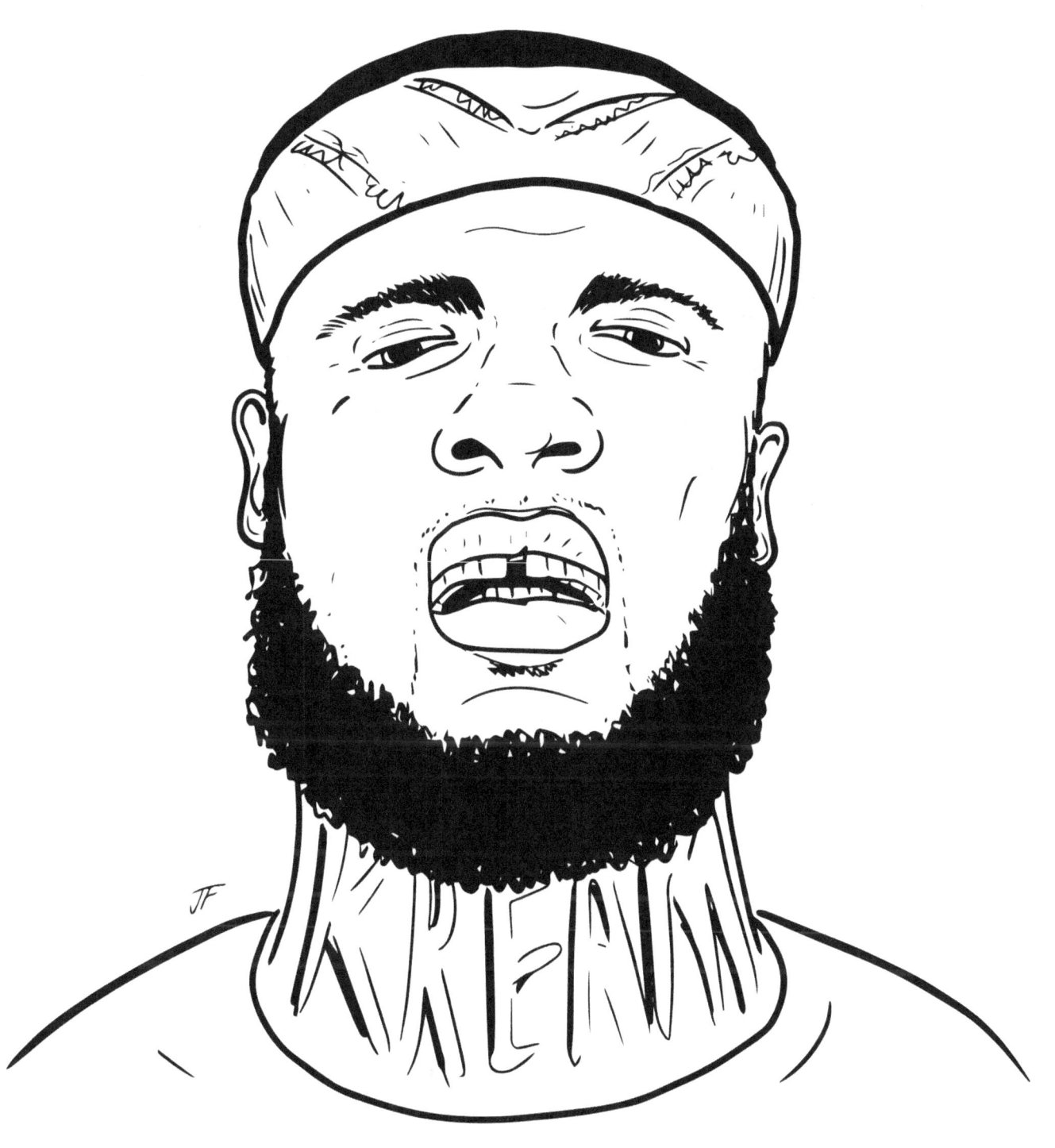

Maxo Kream

About the Creator

Jake Franssen is an American cartoonist, illustrator, and designer. His work has ranged from independently published comic strips, children's books, and graphic novels, to album covers, poster designs, and portraiture. He has worked for music blogs DJBooth.net, Okayplayer.com, and has been published in Highlight's Children's Magazine. He currently resides in Kansas City, Missouri.

Instagram: @thejakefranssen
Twitter: @thejakefranssen

jakefranssen.bigcartel.com

www.ingramcontent.com/pod-product-compliance
Lightning Source LLC
Chambersburg PA
CBHW081421220526
45467CB00009B/2785